Well-behaved women
seldom make history.
—LAUREL THATCHER ULRICH

☆ THE WOMEN WHO BROKE THE RULES SERIES ☆

Judy Blume

Dolley Madison

Sacajawea

Sonia Sotomayor

Coming soon

Coretta Scott King

Mary Todd Lincoln

☆ MORE BOOKS BY KATHLEEN KRULL ☆

A Woman for President

Houdini

Pocahontas

Louisa May's Battle

★ WOMEN WHO ★
★ BROKE THE RULES ★

Sacajawea

KATHLEEN KRULL

interior illustrations by
Matt Collins

BLOOMSBURY

NEW YORK   LONDON   NEW DELHI   SYDNEY

꧁ꕥ꧂

To Dr. Virginia Loh-Hagan,
a woman who breaks the rules

ꞏꕥꞏ

Text copyright © 2015 by Kathleen Krull
Interior illustrations copyright © 2015 by Matt Collins
Cover illustration copyright © 2015 by Edwin Fotheringham

First published in the United States of America in June 2015
by Bloomsbury Children's Books
www.bloomsbury.com

Bloomsbury is a registered trademark of Bloomsbury Publishing Plc

For information about permission to reproduce selections from this book, write to
Permissions, Bloomsbury Children's Books, 1385 Broadway, New York, New York 10018
Bloomsbury books may be purchased for business or promotional use. For information on bulk purchases please contact
Macmillan Corporate and Premium Sales Department at specialmarkets@macmillan.com

Library of Congress Cataloging-in-Publication Data
Krull, Kathleen.
Women who broke the rules : Sacajawea / by Kathleen Krull ; illustrated by Matt Collins.
pages   cm
ISBN 978-0-8027-3800-4 (paperback) • ISBN 978-0-8027-3799-1 (hardcover)
1. Sacagawea—Juvenile literature. 2. Shoshoni women—Biography—Juvenile literature. 3. Shoshoni Indians—Biography—
Juvenile literature. 4. Lewis and Clark Expedition (1804–1806)—Juvenile literature. I. Collins, Matt, illustrator.
II. Title. III. Title: Sacajawea.
F592.7.S123K78 2015   978.0049745740092—dc23   [B]   2014012064

Art created with Prismacolor pencils on vellum with Corel Painter
Typeset in Beaufort
Book design by Nicole Gastonguay

Printed in China by Leo Paper Products, Heshan, Guangdong
2 4 6 8 10 9 7 5 3 1 (paperback)
2 4 6 8 10 9 7 5 3 1 (hardcover)

TABLE OF CONTENTS

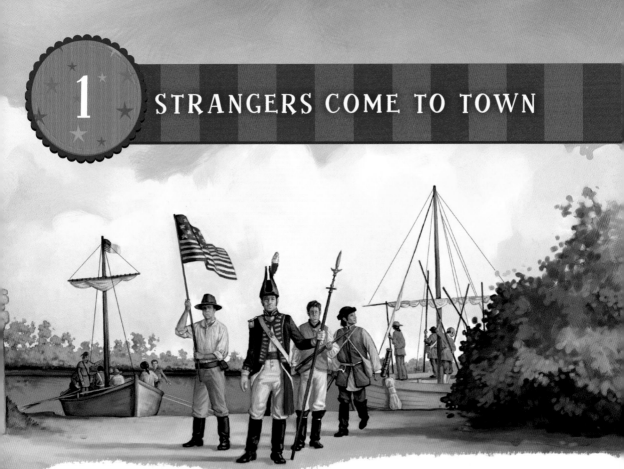

Real-life heroes. Those were the men of the Lewis and Clark mission to explore America. They were also really lucky. Daily they battled death. After a while people back home assumed that death had won.

Besides luck, they had unusual help: a young Shoshone (*Show-SHOW-nee*) Indian woman named Sacajawea (*Sah-cah-jah-WEE-ah*). A real-life heroine. How did she happen to join them?

Alas, the facts about her life are few. Her people had no

written language to tell her story. All we know comes from scribbles in the journals of the men traveling with her. All we know for sure is that her life was unlike that of any other woman of her time. Rules reined women in at every turn. But not Sacajawea.

We think she was born in 1788 in present-day Idaho. Her people were the Lemhi (*LEM-hi*), a band of the Northern Shoshone Indians. Sometimes they were called the Snake Nation because they camped near the Snake River.

Even her name is a mystery. The Lemhi Shoshone prefer "Sacajawea." But the men spelled her name every which way, sometimes giving up and writing "squaw" or "the Indian woman." Meriwether Lewis thought her name meant "bird woman," though historians' opinions differ.

The Shoshone and hundreds of other tribes had lived there for centuries before Europeans arrived. Some people might think of the tribes as being more or less alike. Big mistake. They were different—in languages, traditions, friends, and enemies; how women fared; and how they felt about white settlers.

One Shoshone enemy was the Hidatsa, who sometimes raided them for captives. Although they were skilled horse riders, the Shoshone had trouble beating the gun-wielding Hidatsa using bows and arrows, the Shoshone's only weapons. So they tried to stay out of their enemies' way by living in cold and remote areas. Problem was, not much else lived there, making food scarce. Shoshone lives were harsh, and their search for food simply never ended.

Sacajawea would have been used to constant travel.

Shoshone followed the animals where they roamed and the wild plants as they ripened.

Young Shoshone women seemed to have little say over their lives. Sacajawea would have made clothes and moccasins, prepared and dried fish, collected wood for fires, and made her family's house and kept it repaired.

And what was her reward for all this hard work? She was promised as a bride to a man twice her age. Then in 1800, when she was twelve, the Hidatsa attacked once again. She and her best friend, Jumping Fish, ran to hide in the woods. But warriors spotted them and grabbed them as war prizes.

The girls were taken to live in present-day North Dakota. We know little about these years, except that

Sacajawea mastered the Hidatsa language. Jumping Fish managed to escape. As far as we know Sacajawea didn't try.

Unlike Shoshone women, Hidatsa women helped their economy sizzle. On top of their other duties, they did all the farming. They were able to take their extra corn to trading fairs. In return they got knives, pots, mirrors, guns, and other manufactured goods.

These fairs were also centers for the profitable fur-trading business. Indians trapped and prepared the beautiful furs of otters, foxes, mink, and beavers. The traders at this time were mostly French Canadian, and they were able to sell a wide array of goods. Hidatsa women taught the traders their language, translated for them, and often married them.

At around age fifteen Sacajawea married Toussaint Charbonneau (*Tu-SONT SHAR-ba-no*), a French Canadian trader in his midforties. She might have been sold or traded to him.

One day white strangers arrived in her village.

And she was ready to become part of one of the smartest hiring decisions in history.

Sacajawea was about sixteen and pregnant in November 1804, when she met the men who would change her life.

The year before, President Thomas Jefferson had completed the Louisiana Purchase. This new land, bought from France, more than doubled the size of the United States. Jefferson couldn't wait to turn it into something useful. He hired two of his prized military leaders, Meriwether Lewis, age twenty-nine, and William Clark, age thirty-three, as cocaptains of a complicated mission.

They were to explore, draw maps, study plants and animals, and take lots of notes. The idea was to establish an American claim all the way to the Pacific Ocean. But the main goal was peace—with the Indians and between the tribes who warred with one another. Peace would allow whites to settle the land and get all tribes to trade with them.

Lewis and Clark hired some two dozen men to go along. They had to be in tip-top shape, they had to be good hunters or have some other survival skill, and they needed to be unmarried. The youngest was seventeen, and the oldest was thirty-five. All were paid a monthly salary, except Clark's slave, York. Lewis also brought his Newfoundland dog, Seaman.

The expedition launched from St. Louis in May 1804, as the group sailed up the Missouri River with tons of supplies.

Their first hazard, after five months of fairly smooth travel, was winter. Temperatures plunged to forty-five degrees below zero. Luckily, they had planned to spend winter in the Hidatsa villages. These teeming towns were friendly to whites.

Toussaint Charbonneau, always enterprising, offered his services to the mission. He spoke French and Hidatsa. For five hundred dollars, a lot of money at the time, he could interpret for them. In a sort of two-for-one deal, he offered his wife's services as well. Wives were considered property of their husbands, and it's likely that Sacajawea had no say about the offer.

Sacajawea, her husband pointed out, could translate Shoshone to Hidatsa, which Charbonneau could translate into French for the men who spoke French, who would then translate for the two captains, who spoke only English. Like an elaborate game of Telephone, a lot could get lost in translation. But Lewis and Clark were only too happy to hire them both.

They already knew that the steep Rocky Mountains could possibly stop them from getting to the Pacific. They couldn't exactly cross them by boat. Their only hope was to buy horses from the Shoshone known to be in the area. Some of the men knew crude sign language. But it would take more than sign language to pull this off. Sixteen-year-old Sacajawea was the one who could make it happen.

During the winter of February 1805, she went into labor. She was already considered part of the mission, so Lewis took care of her. To keep their group healthy, he and Clark had studied with top doctors. They knew as much about medicine as anyone—that is, not a great deal.

It was a painful birth, lasting for hours. Lewis finally gave her an Indian remedy, a powder made from a rattlesnake's rattle. Within ten minutes, a healthy baby named Jean Baptiste (*Jhan Ba-TEEST*) was born.

Less than two months later, in April 1805, the mission was on its way.

Was Sacajawea skittish about traveling into the unknown with an infant strapped to her back on a cradle board? Was she scared to be the only woman in a large group of men? We don't know. The men seemed to treat her with respect, calling her "a good creature, of a mild and gentle disposition."

Also, the interpreters were treated like VIPs. They got to live in the captains' quarters, and eat what the captains ate, which was at least one hot meal a day.

With six canoes and two large rowboats, the group

managed fifteen to twenty miles a day. Lewis and Clark took turns walking along the shore, making nature notes. Sacajawea often walked with Clark. Using sign language, she told what she knew about the area, its climate, the plants, and the customs of the local Indians.

It must have bothered her that the men's diets were so very meaty. On the third day, she searched for mouse nests. Mice were known to collect wild artichokes. She dug them up and cooked them for dinner—a surprise that tasted like potatoes.

One day in May, only a month into the trip, a sudden

storm hit the boat carrying the most important supplies. Sacajawea happened to be in the boat with her husband, who was not much of a sailor. The boat started to sink in the rushing waters. Lewis and Clark stood helplessly on the river-bank, shouting instructions to the panicked Charbonneau. Alas, the trader, who couldn't swim, was screaming too loud to hear them.

Lewis got ready to jump in and swim over to take control, even though he knew he'd probably drown. Charbonneau somehow finally steadied the boat. But valuable items had tumbled into the water.

Sacajawea began snatching up medicines, instruments,

books, goods for trading, and most important, the captains'
journals.

Calmly—and with her baby on her back.

Even Lewis, who could be crabby, praised her at length in
his journal. Clark echoed that she had saved "almost every
article necessary to insure the success of the enterprise."

The captains were so grateful that, six days later, they
named a river in her honor. Lewis called it the "bird woman's
river, after our interpreter the Snake woman."

Everyone realized that the mission might have had to
turn back if not for her.

Then, in June, their heroine fell seriously ill. With an infection and a high fever, she rested in a boat, taking care of the baby as best she could.

For the next three weeks, the journey went on, but everyone fretted about her. One of the men wrote a bleak note: "What a great loss she would be."

Clark treated Sacajawea by bloodletting. This popular "remedy" usually made everything worse. Lewis panicked when she started twitching and almost lost her pulse, probably due to blood loss. He dosed her with a mixture of opium and boiled Peruvian bark, the aspirin of its day. It took her weeks to fully recover, but under their close care she grew stronger.

Each day blitzed the mission with challenges. Injuries and illness plagued them. Finding enough food was a daily struggle. Mosquitoes tortured them. They had narrow escapes from mudslides, grizzly bears, and rattlesnakes. The weather was frequently horrible. The worst was a flash flood that almost drowned Sacajawea in a canyon. Her husband and Clark pulled and pushed her and the baby to safety—mostly Clark, as Charbonneau, with his fear of water, wasn't much help.

Every member of the group had a vital role. Lewis's dog, Seaman, for example, caught squirrels and other tasty animals. And his bark served as an alarm when bears or buffalo threatened the camp.

As for Charbonneau, he was better as a cook than a translator. One of the group's favorite meals was his buffalo sausage, made from six feet of buffalo guts. Lewis raved that it was "one of the greatest delicacies of the forest."

Otherwise, Lewis found him a bit clueless. But he put up with him because he needed Sacajawea.

One day Clark wrote in his journal that the trader had struck his wife during dinner. Lewis made a note of it too. At the time, no laws stopped men from hitting their wives. But Clark gave Charbonneau an angry scolding. Some think Charbonneau was a cruel husband, without much evidence besides this.

The baby played a role too. No journal ever mentions a crying or whining infant. For diapers, Sacajawea probably pounded dried buffalo dung into powder, packing a layer of it around the baby. When the layer had absorbed what it needed to, she could toss it and put on another.

The group's youngest member cheered up the weary men. Who doesn't love a little baby, coaxing a smile or a giggle?

He apparently enjoyed the fiddle music that one of the

men played at night, because his nickname became Dancing Boy.

Sacajawea was ever helpful. "In trouble she was full of resources, plucky and determined," Clark wrote.

Again and again, she improved the group's all-meat-all-the-time menu. She found wild berries, dug up roots, and caught fish, adding taste, variety, and vitamins. It's possible she sometimes saved them from starving and prevented fatal illnesses.

But her greatest value may have been simply her calm presence. As Clark pointed out, "A woman with a party of men is a token of peace."

Whenever they met Indians who assumed that this was a war party, the sight of Sacajawea probably kept the men from being killed on the spot.

pproaching the Rocky Mountains, everyone stared up in dread. The peaks rose at least a mile into the sky, topped with deep snow even in summer.

The success of the entire mission depended on having horses to get them and their gear across.

For weeks, they had been traveling almost blindly. But by the end of July 1805, Sacajawea was recognizing places from her childhood. She seemed to have an unusually keen memory, and the exhausted men brightened whenever she could identify anything.

One day in August, not long after she'd fully recovered from her illness, Sacajawea took Lewis's arm. They'd reached Beaverhead Rock, a landmark near where she'd grown up.

She told them which fork of the river to take next. Lewis wrote: "She assures us that we shall either find her people on this river or on the river immediately west." To speed things up, he set off on his own with a few men, leaving Sacajawea behind with Clark's group.

Lewis came upon several Shoshone women. They were clearly terrified. Sacajawea had instructed him to carry a pot of red paint for this very reason. Painting your cheeks with red was a sign of peace. Thanks to this gentle gesture, the women took him to their camp. Some sixty warriors embraced him and his men, smearing them with paint and oil. "I was heartily tired of the national hug," Lewis complained.

Hours later, as Sacajawea approached with Clark, she

rushed ahead, dancing and crying. She stuck two fingers in her mouth and sucked them. Clark recognized this as sign language meaning these were her people. Excellent news.

First she found Jumping Fish, the best friend she'd been captured with. She also saw the man she was supposed to marry—still ready to claim her, until he saw her baby.

Stunning everyone, she recognized the chief. It was none other than her own brother, Cameahwait (*Ca-ME-ah-wate*). With delight she threw a blanket over him and burst into tears. She presented him with a lump of white sugar—the first he'd ever tasted.

Alas, she learned that much of the rest of her family was dead. But the sister-and-brother reunion was mostly a happy occasion. The Shoshone were ready to talk, and she was ready to translate. First there was an elaborate pipe ceremony to establish peace, and then the Indians shared their meager food—cakes made from dried berries.

Negotiations were long and tense. Eventually the mission got the twenty-nine horses they needed, plus a Shoshone guide known as Old Toby.

None of the men who kept journals wrote that Sacajawea showed any desire to stay behind with her people. Her loyalty was to the mission. Why? Leaving Charbonneau probably wasn't even an option. Also, she had enough to eat—at least one hot meal a day—while the Shoshone were starving. Perhaps they now felt like strangers to her. Perhaps the journey lured her on, and she couldn't wait to see the ocean. Or perhaps being treated like a VIP felt good.

They started their painful climb up the steep, rocky slopes. Horses kept slipping, spilling supplies, and sometimes becoming crippled. Men kept falling too.

They soon realized they didn't have enough horses. Luck-ily, they came across a tribe that sold them more. Another tribe helped them with maps and shared its food. Everyone they met was friendly, thanks to Sacajawea.

The crossing was so long and so brutal that at times the group was starving and forced to eat their precious horses to survive.

Finally, by early October, they were heading downhill and looking forward to traveling by water again. The local Indi-ans, the Nez Perce, kindly agreed to care for their surviving horses until they returned.

The only fatalities of the crossing had been the horses. Luck—and Sacajawea—was on Lewis and Clark's side.

They could smell it first, then hear it. Finally, on November 7, they saw it—the Pacific Ocean. Clark wrote, "Ocean in view! O! The Joy!" Actually, it was a branch of the ocean extending into present-day Oregon, but still a relief. After 4,100 miles of travel, they'd reached their goal.

They had to hurry to build camp. Finding a dry site in this rain-soaked area was such a challenge that they decided to hold a vote.

Everyone got to vote—even the teenage girl. "Janey," as

Lewis recorded it, voted for "a place where there is plenty of potas"—the nourishing roots Sacajawea roasted that tasted like potatoes. (Both captains used "Janey" as her nickname.)

Her vote was historic. It would be another 64 years before any state gave women the right to vote, and 115 years before the nation did.

Over the next few weeks, the group built eight small log cabins. As always, the local Indians—the Clapsot—helped them. Sacajawea and her family—the baby was now starting to crawl—again shared Lewis and Clark's cabin.

In all four months there, only fifteen days had sunshine.

Their enemies were hunger and boredom. Sacajawea helped with both. As Clark wrote, "Intelligent, cheerful, tireless, faithful, she inspired us all."

Some days they all had to fast. But even in an area unfamiliar to her, she found fresh roots and berries. She showed the men how to boil elk bones into a grease that could be eaten.

It's possible she also showed them how to make moccasins for the trip back. They went a little overboard—making 358 moccasins, which came to at least ten pairs per person. Whatever befell them, they'd have their feet protected.

The rest of the time, they mended clothes, made salt from the ocean water, and hunted. At night the fiddler brought out his violin and they danced with the Clapsot.

Lewis and Clark hunkered down with their journals. They

recorded hundreds of plants and animals new to science. They drew about 140 maps, including the first accurate maps of the area.

At Christmas, Sacajawea presented Clark with twenty-four white weasel tails she'd been collecting. It was a gift worthy of a great warrior.

Her only recorded complaint of the entire journey came

in January 1806. The Clapsot had told them about a beached whale up the coast. Lewis gathered a crew to go get some of its valuable blubber.

Sacajawea seemed peeved: "She observed," wrote Clark, "that she had traveled a long way with us to see the great waters, and that now that monstrous fish was also to be seen, she thought it very hard that she should not be permitted to see either." That Clark makes such a big deal out of this implies she wasn't ordinarily a whiner.

He wrote that they "indulged" her wishes, and she became part of the crew.

She was probably the first Shoshone Indian to see the ocean. It was a first for all of them. Of all the eye-popping scenery they'd seen, these crashing waves were best: "The grandest and most pleasing prospects which my eyes ever surveyed," marveled Clark, "in my front a boundless ocean."

In March 1806, they packed up and started for home.

By this time the mission had been gone so long that Jefferson and many back home assumed everyone in the group was dead. (Lewis did get shot in the butt by one of his men who mistook him for an elk. Luckily, the wound wasn't life-threatening.) In fact, only one man died, after his appendix burst.

But in May the baby fell ill, with a high fever and swelling—possibly mumps. Everyone ached. No one wanted to lose their little mascot. Clark tried various herbal remedies and finally, after a week, the baby started recovering.

In July, with obvious affection, Clark named a huge rock after the dancing boy, who was sometimes called Pomp. It's now known as Pompey's Pillar National Monument in Montana.

Upon their arrival home the next month, the mission left Sacajawea and her family at the Hidatsa villages and went on to St. Louis. No one recorded anyone's feelings upon the parting.

Clark did sing their guide's praises: "Indeed she has borne with a patience truly admirable the fatigues of so long a route encumbered with an infant, who is even now, only nineteen months old."

With that, Sacajawea starts to fade from the official historical record.

The Lewis and Clark mission changed America forever: fifteen new states were about to be born out of Indian land.

Each captain received a large sum plus 1,600 acres of land. The members were rewarded with 320 acres each, in addition to their monthly salaries. Charbonneau was paid his five hundred dollars. Clark's slave, York, went unpaid, and it was years before he became free.

Clark called Sacajawea "the Indian woman who has been

of great service to me as a pilot through this country." But it never occurred to anyone to pay her. A woman earning her own money? Unheard of!

Clark, at least, felt guilty. As he wrote to Charbonneau, "Your woman who accompanied you that long, dangerous and fatiguing route deserved a greater reward." Clark offered to adopt their son, this "beautiful, promising child." But the baby was too young to leave his mom.

Over the years, Clark kept in touch with his translators. When Jean Baptiste turned six, they finally let Clark adopt him. Sacajawea may never have seen her son again.

Jean Baptiste received the best education money could buy. Sharing his mother's gift for languages, he could speak at least five of them by age eighteen. He became a fur trader and an unusually well-educated mountain man. He died in 1866 at sixty-one in Oregon.

Myths arose about Sacajawea, based on claims by people who said they met her when she was an elderly woman. Some think she eventually left her husband, found her way back to her Shoshone people, and lived to be a well-respected woman of one hundred.

But all the documents point to her death in 1812 in South Dakota. A clerk at Fort Manuel wrote, "This evening the wife of Charbonneau, a Snake squaw, died of a putrid fever. She was a good and the best woman in the fort, aged about twenty-five years. She left a fine infant girl."

This was Lisette. Clark became her guardian too, though it's believed she died as a child.

Charbonneau was off translating at the time of his wife's death. He continued this work and may have lived into his eighties.

In the surge to build America, the Lewis and Clark mission was largely forgotten. In 1902 a romantic novel that included Sacajawea inspired more myths about her.

Two years later, celebrating the hundredth anniversary of the Louisiana Purchase, the World's Fair in St. Louis brought new attention to Lewis and Clark as American heroes.

Sacajawea was also finally getting respect. A hundred years after her journey, women still couldn't vote. But because of her historic vote in Oregon, Susan B. Anthony and other suffragettes used her as a role model. Sacajawea's example proved that all women should be allowed to vote.

No other American woman has had so many rivers and mountains named for her. We have no idea what she looked like, but that hasn't stopped artists from honoring her with statues and paintings. She's usually shown pointing dramatically, something she probably didn't do.

Some Indians view her as a traitor, one who helped the people taking their land. Others have seen her as a source of pride and inspiration.

Year after year children learn about her in school. Sacajawea has been rewarded by becoming legendary as a vital part of American history.

★ SOURCES AND FURTHER READING ★

Books
(* especially for young readers)

Ambrose, Stephen E. *Lewis & Clark: Voyage of Discovery*. Washington, DC: National
    Geographic Society, 1998.

* Berne, Emma Carlson. *Sacagawea: Crossing the Continent with Lewis & Clark*. New York:
    Sterling, 2010.

* Bial, Raymond. *The Shoshone*. New York: Cavendish Square, 2001.

Clark, Ella E., and Margot Edmonds. *Sacagawea of the Lewis and Clark Expedition*. Berkeley:
    University of California Press, 1983.

Danisi, Thomas C., and John C. Jackson. *Meriwether Lewis*. Amherst, NY: Prometheus Books,
    2009.

* DeCapua, Sarah. *The Shoshone*. New York: Cavendish Square, 2007.

Foley, William E. *Wilderness Journey: The Life of William Clark*. Columbia, MO: University of
    Missouri Press, 2004.

Gunderson, Mary. *The Food Journal of Lewis & Clark: Recipes for an Expedition*. Yankton, SD:
    History Cooks, 2002.

Josephy Jr, Alvin M. *Lewis and Clark Through Indian Eyes*. New York: Knopf, 2006.

McIntosh, Elaine N. *The Lewis and Clark Expedition: Food, Nutrition, and Health*. Sioux Falls,
    SD: The Center for Western Studies, Augustana College, 2003.

Morris, Larry E. *The Fate of the Corps: What Became of the Lewis and Clark Explorers After the
    Expedition*. New Haven: Yale University Press, 2004.

* Murphy, Claire Rudolf. *I Am Sacajawea, I Am York: Our Journey West with Lewis and Clark*.
    New York: Walker Children's, 2005.

Ronda, James P. *Lewis & Clark Among the Indians*. Lincoln: University of Nebraska Press, 1984.

* Stille, Darlene R. *The Journals of Lewis and Clark*. Chicago: Heinemann-Raintree, 2012.

Websites

The Journals of the Lewis and Clark Expedition Online: **http://lewisandclarkjournals.unl.edu**

Lemhi-Shoshone Indian Community: **www.lemhi-shoshone.com**

Lewis and Clark: Interactive Journey Log: **www.nationalgeographic.com/lewisandclark**

Lewis and Clark: The Journey of the Corps of Discovery, PBS: **www.pbs.org/lewisandclark**

Lewis and Clark National Historic Trail: **www.nps.gov/lecl/index.htm**

Sacajawea's Home: **http://sacajaweahome.com**

The Shoshone Indians: **http://shoshoneindian.com**

Shoshone-Bannock Tribes Website: **www.shoshonebannocktribes.com**

★ INDEX ★